Intrigue Your Mind
Daily Questions

Book One

Wendi M. Lindenmuth

Also, by Wendi M. Lindenmuth

Dear Lyme Disease: Transforming Your Pain into Purpose

Healing From Within: A Chakra and Ho'oponopono Healing Guidebook

Intrigue Your Mind
Daily Questions

All Rights Reserved

COPYRIGHT © 2024 Wendi M. Lindenmuth

This book may not be reproduced, transmitted, scanned, distributed, or stored in whole or in part by any means, including graphic, electronic, or mechanical, without the publisher's written consent. Thank you for the support of the author's rights.

Paperback ISBN: 978-1-957809-82-3

Hardcover ISBN: 978-1-957809-83-0

Cover Design by Cover Creator

Published by Healing Forward LLC

I love questions.

My entire life, I have been asking questions and questioning everything.

This book contains insightful and fun questions I have asked and engaged thousands of people to help them think outside the box and continue learning more about the world and themselves.

I hope you enjoy it and learn from it, too.

Day 1

An extraordinary attitude can turn an ordinary day into an amazing adventure.

How is your attitude today?

Notes

....
....
....
....
....
....
....
....
....
....
....
....

Day 2

What message do you need to write to yourself today?

Notes

Day 3

How would you describe yourself physically?

Notes

....
....
....
....
....
....
....
....
....
....
....
....

Day 4

How would you describe yourself mentally?

Notes

....
....
....
....
....
....
....
....
....
....
....
....

Day 5

How would you describe yourself emotionally?

Notes

....
....
....
....
....
....
....
....
....
....
....
....

Day 6

How would you describe yourself spiritually?

Notes

Day 7

Do you take the time to focus on what you need most to feel whole and healthy?

If not, how different would you feel if you did?

What are some ways you can start?

Notes

....
....
....
....
....
....
....
....
....
....
....
....
....

Day 8

Have you ever had a near-death experience?
If so, how did it impact your life?

Notes

....
....
....
....
....
....
....
....
....
....
....
....

Day 9

You have one hour left on Earth.

What do you do with that time?

Notes

....
....
....
....
....
....
....
....
....
....
....
....

Day 10

You wake up as a newly formed human. You have memories from your past and your ancestors. You can download qualities, values, and characteristics to help you survive and thrive on Earth. What would they be?

Notes

Day 11

Do you think of pain as your friend or enemy?

Why?

Notes

....
....
....
....
....
....
....
....
....
....
....
....

Day 12

You receive a family toy passed down to each generation's firstborn. The toy has special powers. What kind of toy is it, what are its powers, and how will you use it?

Notes

Day 13

What is your innermost question today?

Notes

Day 14

You develop a gaming device that could improve humanity's future. In the wrong hands, it could impact humankind negatively. What is it? Do you proceed in developing it or keep it a secret?

Notes

Day 15

You suddenly become aware of a shift in the world as it becomes completely silent. What do you imagine happened and why?

Notes

....
....
....
....
....
....
....
....
....
....
....
....

Day 16

What or who helps make you feel your best?

Who do you help feel their best?

Notes

....
....
....
....
....
....
....
....
....
....
....
....

Day 17

Where feels like "home" for you?

Why?

Notes

....
....
....
....
....
....
....
....
....
....
....
....

Day 18

You are part of a group of travelers exploring a deep, dark, remote cave. What did you find that could change the fate of humanity?

Notes

Day 19

You suddenly realize that your survival depends on this one thing. What is it?

Notes

....
....
....
....
....
....
....
....
....
....
....
....

Day 20

What three things would you want to be able to shapeshift into? Why?

Notes

....
....
....
....
....
....
....
....
....
....
....

Day 21

What would you do if you knew your life would drastically change based on your next decision?

Notes

....
....
....
....
....
....
....
....
....
....
....
....

Day 22

You are digging in your backyard and discover a time capsule over 100 years old. What are you surprised to find in it?

Notes

Day 23

You are stranded on a hike when you encounter a tiny cottage in the forest. What and who do you find in there?

What message do they have for you?

Notes

....
....
....
....
....
....
....
....
....
....
....
....

Day 24

Due to a blizzard, you are stuck at your current location. You decide to explore and discover rooms and floors you never knew existed. What do you find?

Notes

....
....
....
....
....
....
....
....
....
....
....
....

Day 25

What will you do with the time that you have today?

Notes

....
....
....
....
....
....
....
....
....
....
....
....

Day 26

You wake up and can't remember your past. Do you try to discover who you are, create a new identity, and live a new life?

Notes

Day 27

How do you decide where to go when you find yourself at a crossroads in life?

Notes

....
....
....
....
....
....
....
....
....
....
....
....

Day 28

What are you waiting for?

How much longer are you going to wait?

Notes

....
....
....
....
....
....
....
....
....
....
....

Day 29

Amid a creative block, you take a walk for inspiration but get lost and get more than you bargained for. What happened?

Notes

....
....
....
....
....
....
....
....
....
....
....
....
....

Day 30

If you were a tree, what kind would you be, why, and where would you like to be planted?

Notes

....
....
....
....
....
....
....
....
....
....
....
....

Day 31

You are in a waiting room in a clinic that promises to cure whatever you need. As you wait, you begin to get suspicious when you notice this. What is it?

Notes

Day 32

How do you handle criticism? If not well, what can you do to see it differently?

Notes

Day 33

What is there not enough of in your life? What is there too much of in your life?

Notes

....
....
....
....
....
....
....
....
....
....
....
....

Day 34

The more you ignore your inner voice, the harder it will be to hear it when you need it most. Are you quieting the noise around and inside you to listen to the message you need to hear?

What is your message?

Notes

....
....
....
....
....
....
....
....
....
....
....

Day 35

What songs are on your zombie-apocalypse soundtrack?

Notes

....
....
....
....
....
....
....
....
....
....
....
....

Day 36

If you were a flavor, what would you be?

Why?

Notes

....
....
....
....
....
....
....
....
....
....
....
....

Day 37

What musician or song do you think of when you think of LOVE?

Notes

....
....
....
....
....
....
....
....
....
....
....
....

Day 38

What is something others wouldn't believe about you? Why?

Notes

....
....
....
....
....
....
....
....
....
....
....

Day 39

If you were a different species for the whole day, what would you choose, and what would you do?

Notes

Day 40

If you were a chair, what type would you be, and who would you like to sit on you?

Notes

....
....
....
....
....
....
....
....
....
....
....
....

Day 41

How many nicknames do you have? What is your favorite and why?

Notes

....
....
....
....
....
....
....
....
....
....
....

Day 42

What kind would you be if you were a pair of shoes or boots?

Why?

Notes

Day 43

If you could have a song play every time you enter a room, what would it be?

Notes

....
....
....
....
....
....
....
....
....
....
....

Day 44

What do you think your 10-year-old self would tell you right now? Would you listen?

Notes

Day 45

If you were a song, what type of song would you be, and what would be the title?

Notes

....
....
....
....
....
....
....
....
....
....
....
....

Day 46

You wake up discovering you are growing a second head on one of your shoulders. Do you think you would get along? What would you name it?

Notes

Day 47

What book do you wish you could enter, become one of the characters, and be part of the story?

Notes

Day 48

What does your laugh sound like? How often do you laugh?

Notes

Day 49

Where would you want to land if you were a snowflake, and why?

Notes

Day 50

If you could only bring three books with you to read for the rest of your life, what would they be?

Notes

....
....
....
....
....
....
....
....
....
....
....

Day 51

What three items would you bring with you to live on another planet?

Notes

....
....
....
....
....
....
....
....
....
....
....
....

Day 52

If you were a book, what would you be made from?

How old would you be?

Who would you hope would read you, hold you, and understand you?

Notes

....
....
....
....
....
....
....
....
....
....
....

Day 53

If you were a record, who would you hope would play you and dance to your songs?

What kind of songs would be on there?

Notes

....
....
....
....
....
....
....
....
....
....
....
....

Day 54

If you were a pair of socks, whose feet would you want to be on, and what type would you be?

Notes

Day 55

Would you rather own a dragon or be a dragon? Why?

Notes

....
....
....
....
....
....
....
....
....
....
....
....

Day 56

What are a few of your "weaknesses" that you can see as strengths and opportunities?

Notes

Day 57

Have you ever displayed remarkable sangfroid when everyone else was panicking? What was the situation?

Notes

....
....
....
....
....
....
....
....
....
....
....
....

Day 58

If there were no consequences for a day, what would you do?

Notes

....
....
....
....
....
....
....
....
....
....
....
....

Day 59

Would you rather be able to play every musical instrument or speak every language fluently? Why?

Notes

Day 60

Are you aware of how much power your words have?
How can your words have a positive impact today?

Notes

....

....

....

....

....

....

....

....

....

....

....

....

Day 61

What would be on the soundtrack if someone was filming your life up to this point?

Notes

Day 62

If you were an amusement park ride, which would best reflect you and why?

Notes

....
....
....
....
....
....
....
....
....
....
....

Day 63

If you could shoot one condiment from your belly button, what would it be and why?

Notes

....
....
....
....
....
....
....
....
....
....
....
....

Day 64

Do you still have a childhood toy or remember one?
What is it? What memories do you have of it?

Notes

Day 65

What would your ideal secret hideout look like? Who would be allowed in it?

Notes

....
....
....
....
....
....
....
....
....
....
....
....

Day 66

What lifetime supply of something do you want to win? Why?

Notes

Day 67

What are you currently doing to better the world?

Notes

....
....
....
....
....
....
....
....
....
....
....
....
....

Day 68

How would you react if you could read everyone's mind? What would you do with the information you knew?

Notes

Day 69

If you could trade body parts for ones that worked better, which would you choose? What would you do with a functional body?

Notes

Day 70

What was the most memorable thing about your day today?

Notes

Day 71

What do you like most about where you live? Why?

Notes

Day 72

What are you noticing today? Do you like or dislike what you are seeing?

Notes

Day 73

If you could paint the world with your favorite colors, what colors would you choose? Why?

Notes

Day 74

What are you concerned about this week? Why?

Notes

....
....
....
....
....
....
....
....
....
....
....

Day 75

If you were a kitchen appliance, which one would you be and why?

Notes

....
....
....
....
....
....
....
....
....
....
....
....

Day 76

If you could offer a newborn child only one piece of advice, what would it be?

Notes

Day 77

Would you reduce your life expectancy by ten years to become extremely attractive or famous? Why or why not?

Notes

Day 78

What would it be if you could only say one word for the rest of your life?

Notes

....
....
....
....
....
....
....
....
....
....
....

Day 79

What is your innermost desire while you are here on Earth? Why?

Notes

Day 80

You can only wear one outfit for the rest of your life; what would you wear and why?

Notes

Day 81

What can you start eliminating from your life TODAY
that is not serving you for the highest good?

Notes

....
....
....
....
....
....
....
....
....
....
....
....

Day 82

At this moment, right now, what are you hoping for and why?

Notes

....
....
....
....
....
....
....
....
....
....
....

Day 83

When was the last time someone described you as happy?
If it has been a while, can you change that?

Notes

....
....
....
....
....
....
....
....
....
....
....
....
....

Day 84

How is your relationship with money? Are you best friends? Enemies? Lovers? Acquaintances?

Notes

Day 85

Are you addicted to discomfort? If so, how?

Notes

Day 86

When was the last time you laughed so hard you peed yourself?

Notes

....
....
....
....
....
....
....
....
....
....
....
....

Day 87

If you had a music band, what would you name it and why?

Notes

....
....
....
....
....
....
....
....
....
....
....
....

Day 88

As of right now, if you were to die, what legacy would you leave?

Notes

Day 89

What's the first thing you do when you are bored?

Notes

....
....
....
....
....
....
....
....
....
....
....
....

Day 90

Who would you be if you were a character in The Three Little Pigs?

Notes

....
....
....
....
....
....
....
....
....
....
....
....

Day 91

What colors would you choose for each finger if your fingers were crayons?

Notes

Day 92

What do you do when life feels so heavy and is just too much?

Notes

Day 93

What topic do you REALLY want to talk or write about, but you are afraid to or don't feel qualified to do so?

Notes

Day 94

What is the most memorable haircut or style you ever had? I had a haircut like Prince in 10th grade!

Notes

Day 95

What famous art piece would you want to hang in your home and why? Where would you hang it and why?

Notes

....
....
....
....
....
....
....
....
....
....
....

Day 96

What special moments or experiences remind you of the miracles that happen every day?

Notes

....
....
....
....
....
....
....
....
....
....
....
....

Day 97

What was your first thought when you woke up this morning?

Notes

Day 98

Who in your life makes you feel like the most important person in the room?

Who do you make feel like the most important person in the room?

Notes

Day 99

Have you complimented someone today? How did it make them feel? How did it make you feel?

Notes

....
....
....
....
....
....
....
....
....
....
....
....

Day 100

Where do unused dreams go? What dreams do you still have?

Notes

Day 101

How many different personalities does it feel like you have? Do you get along with them?

Notes

Day 102

What piece of wisdom can you share with someone today?

Notes

Day 103

Have you experienced a traumatic event that changed your life for the better? What was it and how?

Notes

Day 104

What areas in your life fill you with the most doubt?
What has helped you overcome this?

Notes

Day 105

What device would you create to improve your life and others? How would it improve it?

Notes

....
....
....
....
....
....
....
....
....
....
....
....

Day 106

What are you avoiding today? Why?

Notes

....
....
....
....
....
....
....
....
....
....
....
....

Day 107

When you quiet the chatter in your head, what do you hear?

Notes

....
....
....
....
....
....
....
....
....
....
....
....

Day 108

Do you sometimes feel more or less evolved than other people? If so, how does that make you feel?

Notes

Day 109

What would you want to be made into if you were a lump of clay? Why?

Notes

....
....
....
....
....
....
....
....
....
....
....
....
....

Day 110

What is something you wish you didn't know? Why?

Notes

Dai 111

What and who are the blessings in your life?

Notes

....
....
....
....
....
....
....
....
....
....
....
....

Day 112

What's the strangest game you used to play as a kid or as an adult?

Notes

....
....
....
....
....
....
....
....
....
....
....
....

Day 113

What is your favorite possession? Why?

Notes

....
....
....
....
....
....
....
....
....
....
....
....

Day 114

How would you react if you lived in a bunker all of your life and were introduced to the world above?

Notes

....
....
....
....
....
....
....
....
....
....
....
....

Day 115

What are your olfactory pleasures? Why those?

Notes

Day 116

What is your relationship with serenity?

Notes

Day 117

What will you never apologize for? Why?

Notes

....
....
....
....
....
....
....
....
....
....
....
....

Day 118

What are you washing your hands of? Why?

Notes

Day 119

How much of your life are you missing out on by not paying attention?

Notes

Day 120

What do you need to unlearn?

Notes

Day 121

What was the most delicious thing you ate recently?

Notes

Day 122

What is the fuel that propels you to achieve your goals and dreams?

Notes

Day 123

What story do you want to tell? Will you? When?

Notes

....
....
....
....
....
....
....
....
....
....
....
....

Day 124

When our bodies aren't at peace, everything can feel like turmoil. How can you start bringing peace into your life?

Notes

Day 125

What could be designed smarter? How would you design it?

Notes

....
....
....
....
....
....
....
....
....
....
....
....

Day 126

What would be your news headline for today?

Notes

Day 127

What could you be a mascot for? Why?

Notes

Day 128

Is there a connection between your losses and wanting to blame others for them?

Notes

Day 129

How do you find your strength each day?

Notes

....
....
....
....
....
....
....
....
....
....
....
....

Day 130

What would you wait an inordinate amount of time for? Why?

Notes

Day 131

What is improving in your life?

Notes

Day 132

If you had a key to unlock ANYTHING, what would it open?

Notes

Day 133

How does magic play a role in your life?

Notes

Day 134

How often do you stand in awe for just waking up each day?

Notes

Day 135

What is something new to add to your to-do list this week?

Notes

....
....
....
....
....
....
....
....
....
....
....
....

Day 136

What do you do to help your faith not to waiver?

Notes

....
....
....
....
....
....
....
....
....
....
....
....

Day 137

Do you feel safe to be yourself? Why or why not?

Notes

Day 138

What would you never open? Why?

Notes

Day 139

What are you craving today?

Notes

Day 140

What is your relationship with compulsion?

Notes

Day 141

What do you do when the things you love to do most start becoming monotonous?

Notes

....
....
....
....
....
....
....
....
....
....
....
....

Day 142

What are you shamelessly persistent about?

Notes

Day 143

What are you searching for today?

Notes

....
....
....
....
....
....
....
....
....
....
....
....

Day 144

Are you confused about your beliefs? Why?

Notes

Day 145

What do you know for certain?

Notes

....
....
....
....
....
....
....
....
....
....
....
....

Day 146

What is your soul song today?

Notes

Day 147

What is your experience with wonderment?

Notes

Day 148

What do you have the capacity to do today? Will you do it?

Notes

Day 149

How are you being kind to yourself today?

Notes

....
....
....
....
....
....
....
....
....
....
....
....

Day 150

What are you contemplating today?

Notes

....
....
....
....
....
....
....
....
....
....
....

Day 151

Are you wearing your scars proudly? What are they?

Notes

Day 152

Is it acceptable to believe that what may seem true one moment may appear otherwise the next? Do you have an example?

Notes

Day 153

What is your relationship with responsibility?

Notes

Day 154

What takes too much brain power?

Notes

Day 155

What are you suffused with?

Notes

....
....
....
....
....
....
....
....
....
....
....
....

Day 156

What is the most audacious thing you have done or said?

Notes

Day 157

What is something you probably shouldn't be doing but will do anyway?

Notes

Day 158

What is something you can't unsee?

Notes

Day 159

What wouldn't you want to claim? Why?

Notes

Day 160

Do you believe healing can spread through time, space, and lineage? Do you have an example?

Notes

Day 161

What would you want to be a witness to?

Notes

....
....
....
....
....
....
....
....
....
....
....
....

Day 162

What wouldn't you want to be a witness to?

Notes

Day 163

Are you investing in continuous learning? Why or why not?

Notes

Day 164

At this very moment, do you love yourself? Why or why not?

Notes

Day 165

Do you think deep within us, we truly know all the answers?

Notes

....
....
....
....
....
....
....
....
....
....
....
....

Day 166

What area of your life do you need to work on the most? Will you?

Notes

Day 167

Does gratitude matter to you? Why or why not?

Notes

Day 168

What have you learned so far today or this week?

Notes

....
....
....
....
....
....
....
....
....
....
....
....

Day 169

How well is your navigational system working?

Notes

....
....
....
....
....
....
....
....
....
....
....
....
....

Day 170

How is your attitude to curiosity?

Notes

Day 171

What do you do when your boundaries are being encroached on?

Notes

....
....
....
....
....
....
....
....
....
....
....
....

Day 172

Do you ever wonder how many more geniuses, artists, composers, scientists, musicians, and so on there would be in the world if we all had someone to spark the potential within us?

Notes

Day 173

As you get older, what are you less of? More of?

Notes

Day 174

What new door are you opening today? Which one are you closing?

Notes

Day 175

Do you ever get caught up in a Maelstrom of emotions?
What helps you?

Notes

Day 176

Are you willing to take a risk today? What will it be?

Notes

Day 177

Which kitchen utensil do you feel most like today? Why?

Notes

Day 178

What were you surprised to do today or this week?

Notes

....
....
....
....
....
....
....
....
....
....
....
....

Day 179

Do you ever feel like time leaves you standing there unsure what to do? Is there anything you can do about it?

Notes

Day 180

Is "time" a friend of yours? Why or why not?

Notes

....
....
....
....
....
....
....
....
....
....
....
....

Day 181

What is your relationship with wisdom?

Notes

Day 182

Can you see clearly which expectations are yours and which belong to someone else?

Notes

Day 183

What are you faking? Why?

Notes

....
....
....
....
....
....
....
....
....
....
....
....

Day 184

If you receive a package that says OPEN IMMEDIATELY, do you? Or do you wait?

Notes

....
....
....
....
....
....
....
....
....
....
....

Day 185

What if you never find the answer you are searching for?

Notes

....
....
....
....
....
....
....
....
....
....
....
....

Day 186

Do we need to find meaning in change and any suffering it may bring?

Notes

....
....
....
....
....
....
....
....
....
....
....
....

Day 187

Do you know your values, or are you still discovering them?

Notes

....
....
....
....
....
....
....
....
....
....
....
....
....

Day 188

What can you learn from a broken mirror?

Notes

Day 189

When do you feel most empowered? Why?

Notes

Day 190

Can you find a reason to dance today?

Notes

....
....
....
....
....
....
....
....
....
....
....
....

Day 191

What is the weirdest urge you have had?

Did you do it?

Notes

....
....
....
....
....
....
....
....
....
....
....
....

Day 192

What is your relationship with challenges?

Notes

Day 193

Why do you think people (not everyone) listen to other people's truth and try to make it our own?

Notes

Day 194

What is your life built on?

Notes

Day 195

At this moment in time, can you accept that you are wonderful the way you are? Why or why not?

Notes

Day 196

What new thing can you explore today or this week?

Notes

Day 197

How are you reconnecting with what inspires you?

Notes

Day 198

How do you want to feel right now? What will it take to feel that way?

Notes

Day 199

Do you believe how you see life is how life will see you?

Notes

Day 200

What would be nice right now?

Notes

Day 201

What would you consider extraneous in your life?

Notes

Day 202

What do you feel painfully aware of?

Notes

....
....
....
....
....
....
....
....
....
....
....
....

Day 203

What do you feel excitingly aware of?

Notes

Day 204

What kind of nugget are you?

Notes

Day 205

Is there a heavy thought that you are stubbornly holding onto? Why?

Notes

....
....
....
....
....
....
....
....
....
....
....
....
....

Day 206

Is there a lighter way to think about what you are thinking about?

Notes

....
....
....
....
....
....
....
....
....
....
....

Day 207

What grade would you give yourself today? Do you need extra credit?

Notes

Day 208

What does no one talk about anymore? Why do you think that is?

Notes

Day 209

How aligned are you with love in your life?

Notes

Day 210

What has taken you longer to do than most people?

Notes

Day 211

If you could make reservations anywhere, where would you choose and why?

Notes

....
....
....
....
....
....
....
....
....
....
....
....

Day 212

What is your pain threshold?

Notes

Day 213

Are you living like you are dying or thriving?

Notes

....
....
....
....
....
....
....
....
....
....
....
....

Day 214

Do you live a carefully curated life? If not, would you want to?

Notes

Day 215

Where there is fear, there is your task. What do you think or feel about this saying?

Notes

....
....
....
....
....
....
....
....
....
....
....

Day 216

How has your current or past pet helped you heal?

Notes

....
....
....
....
....
....
....
....
....
....
....
....

Day 217

Why do you REALLY want what you want?

Notes

Day 218

Do you feel the more you accumulate, the more lost you feel? Why?

Notes

....
....
....
....
....
....
....
....
....
....
....
....

Day 219

How often have you taken the long way to find the shortcut?

Notes

....
....
....
....
....
....
....
....
....
....
....
....

Day 220

What does a life well lived look and feel like to you?

Notes

....
....
....
....
....
....
....
....
....
....
....
....

Day 221

Are you in love with life today? Can you try if you aren't?

Notes

....
....
....
....
....
....
....
....
....
....
....
....

Day 222

If you came with a warning sign, what would it say?

Notes

....
....
....
....
....
....
....
....
....
....
....
....

Day 223

Do you feel like you are putting yourself at risk by letting others see the "real" you? Why?

Notes

....
....
....
....
....
....
....
....
....
....
....
....
....

Day 224

Do you think real tolerance is rooted in empathy?

Notes

Day 225

Are you making allowances for the loved ones in your life?

Notes

Day 226

What are you afraid of forgetting?

Notes

Day 227

What are you having withdrawal symptoms from?

Notes

Day 228

What would be the weirdest thing to happen to you today?

Notes

....
....
....
....
....
....
....
....
....
....
....
....

Day 220

What do you need more of? Why?

Notes

Day 230

What do you need less of? Why?

Notes

Day 23

Do you have the "Someday" Syndrome?

Notes

Day 232

Is happiness tied to honesty? Why or why not?

Notes

Day 233

What kind of crazy are you?

Notes

Day 234

What and who do you need to unsubscribe from today?

Notes

Day 235

Who or what is no longer serving you and helping you be the best version of yourself?

What can you do about it?

Notes

Day 236

What have you circumvented recently?

Notes

Day 237

If you have ever forgiven someone, how did you feel afterward?

Notes

Day 238

Is sharing what you have learned to help others grow easy or difficult?

Notes

Day 239

Are you spending more time thinking about everything you did wrong or right? Why?

Notes

....
....
....
....
....
....
....
....
....
....
....
....

Day 240

Do you think our culture admonishes us to be self-reliant, independent, and strong?

Notes

Day 241

What is sacred to you? Why?

Notes

Day 242

What is your mind giving birth to?

Notes

Day 243

How are you nurturing your relationships with the people you love?

Notes

Day 244

What do you have a voracity for?

Notes

Day 245

What are you NOT?

Notes

Day 246

What state of mind are you in? How did you get there?

Notes

....
....
....
....
....
....
....
....
....
....
....

Day 247

What do you wish you had a list of?

Notes

....
....
....
....
....
....
....
....
....
....
....
....

Day 248

Are you the boss of your life? Why or why not?

Notes

Day 249

Do you feel in charge of your choices today? Why or why not?

Notes

Day 250

Can you risk believing in yourself, something, or someone today?

Notes

Day 251

What opportunities are you appreciating today?

Notes

Day 252

Have you ever felt an eerie and portentous stillness?
What did you do?

Notes

....
....
....
....
....
....
....
....
....
....
....
....

Day 253

Are you boldly asking the universe (or higher spirit) for what you want? Why or why not?

Notes

....
....
....
....
....
....
....
....
....
....
....
....
....

Day 254

What are some practical ways to show love? Are you doing this?

Notes

Day 255

If you had scheduled updates, what would you be updated with?

Notes

Day 256

Why are you waiting to make needed changes when any moment may be your last?

Notes

Day 257

Is how we feel and think about others tied to how we feel and think about ourselves?

Notes

Day 258

What are you trying to make happen instead of allowing it to unfold organically?

Notes

....
....
....
....
....
....
....
....
....
....
....
....

Day 259

What have you learned from your relationship with trees?

Notes

Day 260

What have you learned from your relationship with nature?

Notes

Day 261

What are you standing up for today?

Notes

Day 262

What is your relationship with hindsight?

Notes

Day 263

What have you learned from your relationship with animals?

Notes

Day 264

Where is your internal GPS leading you?

Notes

Day 265

When was the last time you observed a child and noticed how they approached things with such simplicity? Would your outlook change if you approached life the same way?

Notes

....
....
....
....
....
....
....
....
....
....
....

Day 266

Do you think wisdom helps us not judge but love and nurture?

Notes

Day 267

What or who in your life brings you the most joy?

Notes

....
....
....
....
....
....
....
....
....
....
....

Day 268

How are you keeping your sources of healing and energy fed?

Notes

Day 269

Can you be happy even if you don't get what you want?

Notes

Day 270

Do you think we only genuinely appreciate someone or something once it is gone?

Notes

Day 271

Do you think it's better to risk saying too much than holding back due to fear? What has been your experience?

Notes

....
....
....
....
....
....
....
....
....
....
....
....

Day 272

Are you complicating your life by trying to figure everything out? How can you focus on one thing at a time?

Notes

Day 273

How are you celebrating YOU this week?

Notes

....
....
....
....
....
....
....
....
....
....
....
....

Day 274

What is your relationship with nepotism?

Notes

Day 275

In what areas of your life does your mind need to be renewed?

Notes

Day 276

What do you wish you had a pocketful of? Why?

Notes

Day 277

What has been your biggest irony in life? Why?

Notes

Day 278

Are you expressing appreciation for the loved ones in your life?

Notes

....
....
....
....
....
....
....
....
....
....
....
....

Day 279

When you are lonely, what do you try to do or think about to help you?

Notes

....
....
....
....
....
....
....
....
....
....
....
....

Day 280

How will you enhance your growth today?

Notes

Day 281

Are you open to exploring the elements of your unconsciousness?

Notes

Day 282

How often do you contemplate your existence?

Notes

Day 283

What odd thing has become habit-forming for you?

Notes

Day 284

How are you girding up your mind?

Notes

Day 285

If you could create any festival, what theme would it be and where?

Notes

Day 286

How often do you reflect on your accomplishments?
What are they?

Notes

Day 287

How naughty have you been today?

Notes

....
....
....
....
....
....
....
....
....
....
....
....

Day 288

How often do you reflect on your regrets? Why?

Notes

Day 289

If you have been unsatisfied with your life, what do you think the root cause is?

Notes

....
....
....
....
....
....
....
....
....
....
....
....

Day 290

What would it be if you were stuck doing only one activity for the rest of your life?

Notes

....
....
....
....
....
....
....
....
....
....
....
....

Day 291

Do you think our experiences are enriched when we view them with new attitudes?

Notes

Day 292

Are you living your best day today? Why or why not?

Notes

Day 293

What is the key to sustained growth?

Notes

Day 294

What are you attaching your worthiness or your identity to? Why?

Notes

Day 295

What is your spirit singing today?

Notes

Day 296

What are you doing to show love and kindness to others?

Notes

Day 297

Who is your alter ego? By what name do you call it?

Notes

....
....
....
....
....
....
....
....
....
....
....
....

Day 298

What has been a harbinger in your life? Why?

Notes

Day 299

Who or what do you wish you could squeeze right now? Why?

Notes

Day 300

What is the most important advice you have received and followed about any subject since your time on Earth?

Notes

Day 301

What is your relationship with synchronicity?

Notes

Day 302

If you were a billboard, what would your message be, and what would the picture be?

Notes

Day 303

How easy is it for you to believe the best in a person? Why?

Notes

....
....
....
....
....
....
....
....
....
....
....
....

Day 304

Do you love yourself for being unique or worry about being different from everyone else?

Notes

....
....
....
....
....
....
....
....
....
....
....

Day 305

Did you find anything today? What?

Notes

....
....
....
....
....
....
....
....
....
....
....
....

Day 306

What role are you fulfilling today?

Notes

Day 307

Do you believe we are all here on Earth with a specific assignment? What is yours?

Notes

....
....
....
....
....
....
....
....
....
....
....
....

Day 308

What is one thing you really need to tell someone today? Will you?

Notes

Day 309

In the midst of havoc, can you find the stillness?

Notes

Day 310

How are you limiting and protecting yourself from information overload?

Notes

Day 311

Do you recognize the importance of rest? How will you honor your rest?

Notes

Day 312

When was the last time you took a moment to notice a loved one's face and the sound of their voice?

Notes

Day 313

Are you conscious of the direction you're going towards?

Notes

Day 314

What do you do when you encounter someone who is disingenuous?

Notes

Day 315

What is your gut telling you? Are you listening?

Notes

Day 316

What song are your bones singing today?

Notes

....
....
....
....
....
....
....
....
....
....
....
....

Day 317

Do you think we are all just trying to survive until someone comes to rescue us?

Notes

Day 318

If your need to give love exceeds others to receive it, what do you do?

Notes

Day 319

Can you look yourself in the mirror at the end of day and day and like what you see?

Notes

Day 320

What do you think your main lesson(s) here on Earth have been?

Notes

....
....
....
....
....
....
....
....
....
....
....
....

Day 321

What part of your body feels the most scared right now? Do you know why?

Notes

Day 322

What is your relationship with envy?

Notes

Day 323

What would it feel like if what you desired and wanted was here right now?

Notes

....
....
....
....
....
....
....
....
....
....
....
....

Day 324

What do you care about today?

Notes

....
....
....
....
....
....
....
....
....
....
....
....

Day 325

Do you believe the essence of humanity lies in our ability to serve and give to others?

Notes

Day 326

Do you continuously place unrealistic demands on yourself? How can you stop doing that?

Notes

Day 327

Do you believe we are truly here on a spiritual quest? What is yours?

Notes

Day 328

Do you ever get surprised discovering the strength within you to accomplish something?

Notes

Day 329

What do you feel is lackluster in your life? How will you change that?

Notes

....
....
....
....
....
....
....
....
....
....
....
....

Day 330

Are you doing what makes your soul happy? Why or why not?

Notes

Day 331

What is your relationship with curiosity?

Notes

Day 332

What is one of the first steps to a better life?

Notes

Day 333

What activity have you been so engrossed in that changed the perception of time?

Notes

………………………………………………………………………………………………
………………………………………………………………………………………………
………………………………………………………………………………………………
………………………………………………………………………………………………
………………………………………………………………………………………………
………………………………………………………………………………………………
………………………………………………………………………………………………
………………………………………………………………………………………………
………………………………………………………………………………………………
………………………………………………………………………………………………
………………………………………………………………………………………………
………………………………………………………………………………………………

Day 334

What tools do you use to weed out unhealthy messages from your subconscious?

Notes

Day 335

Are you checking the weather inside your heart? What is it?

Notes

Day 336

Can you use your imagination to shape the person you yearn to be?

Notes

Day 337

How do you identify when your intuition is trying to keep you safe versus when your fears are trying to keep you small?

Notes

Day 338

What do you think has helped you deal with difficult situations healthily?

Notes

Day 339

Do you require empirical proof to believe something? If so, like what?

Notes

Day 340

What do you think has hindered your healing?

Notes

....
....
....
....
....
....
....
....
....
....
....
....

Day 341

When was the last time you felt a frisson of delight?

Notes

Day 342

Do you feel empowered when you speak from your own center?

Notes

Day 343

Are you listening to your body? What is it telling you?

Notes

Day 344

Non-resistance is refreshing. What is your relationship with resistance?

Notes

Day 345

What are you an unofficial doctor of?

Notes

Day 346

How much do you really think other people influence what you believe?

Notes

Day 347

How often do you do a self-assessment?

Notes

Day 348

What are you a plethora of?

Notes

Day 349

Why do "we" try to be so busy that somehow, we hope to anesthetize ourselves and not hurt so much?

Notes

Day 350

Do you have the patience and awareness to see everyone in your life as a potential teacher?

Notes

Day 351

What would be difficult for you to walk away from? Why?

Notes

Day 352

What are you exemplary in?

Notes

Day 353

How different would your life be if you saw everyone you met worthy of love and respect?

Notes

Day 354

What took a lot of gumption for you to do?

Notes

Day 355

What is an unaddressed pain within you?

Notes

Day 356

What do you think will happen the moment you stop waiting for other things to occur?

Notes

Day 357

What is your relationship with disappointment?

Notes

Day 358

To whom can you give a compliment today?

Notes

Day 359

What are you allowing your ego free reign to?

Notes

Day 360

What is your favorite thing about being human?

Notes

Day 361

What experience(s) do you hunger for?

Notes

Day 362

Your attitude is your window to the world. How is your attitude today?

Notes

Day 363

What is your relationship with equanimity?

Notes

Day 364

What are you trying to resolve?

Notes

....
....
....
....
....
....
....
....
....
....
....
....

Day 365

Do you ever feel that you encourage conflicts?

Notes

Day 366

What needs to be changed in your life? Can you accomplish that?

Notes

....
....
....
....
....
....
....
....
....
....
....

Thank you for reading and engaging in all my questions.

Please stay in touch.

Website: https://www.healingforwardwithwendi.com/

Twitter: https://twitter.com/LindenmuthWendi

Thank you!

Wendi